LEGAL
COUNSEL

NATIONAL LIBRARY OF CANADA CATALOGUING IN PUBLICATION DATA

Vandor, Les
Legal counsel: frequently asked questions about the law

Contents: bk. 1. An introduction to the legal system, individual rights and
employment rights bk. 2. Property rights, family and divorce and company
rights bk. 3. Retirement, representation and wills bk. 4. Criminal law

ISBN 1-55022-483-2 V.1. ISBN 1-55022-485-9 V.2.
ISBN 1-55022-486-7 V.3. ISBN 1-55022-553-7 V.4.

1. Law Canada – Popular works. 1. Title.

KE447.V35 2001   349.71   C2001-900823-6

Author photo on back cover by Marilyn Mikkelsen
Cover and text design by Tania Craan
Layout by Wiesia Kolasinska

Printed by Transcontinental

Distributed in Canada by
Jaguar Book Group
100 Armstrong Avenue
Georgetown, ON L7G 5S4

Published by ECW PRESS
2120 Queen Street East, Suite 200
Toronto, ON M4E 1E2
ecwpress.com

This book is set in Bembo and Futura.

PRINTED AND BOUND IN CANADA

The publication of *Legal Counsel* has been generously supported by the
Government of Canada through the Book Publishing
Industry Development Program. Canadä

Disclaimer: The questions and answers that follow are meant as a guide.
You are encouraged to consult with your own legal practitioner for
details as to your particular situation.

LEGAL COUNSEL

FREQUENTLY ASKED
QUESTIONS
ABOUT THE LAW

BOOK FOUR

Criminal Law

LES VANDOR, QC

ECW PRESS

To you for your questions

TABLE OF CONTENTS

FOREWORD by the Hon. Allan McEachern, former Chief Justice of British Columbia

FOREWORD by the Hon. Lorne Clarke, former Chief Justice of Nova Scotia

PREFACE

INTRODUCTION

INTRODUCTION TO THE CRIMINAL CODE

PART 1: The General Rules   3

PART 2: Offences against Public Order   6

PART 3: Firearms   12

PART 4: Offences against the Administration of Justice   17

PART 5: Sexual Offences   21

PART 6: Privacy   23

PART 7: Gaming and Prostitution   25

PART 8: Offences against the Person   28

PART 9: Property   35

PART 10: Fraud   37

PARTS 11 and 12: Forbidden Property Acts and Currency   40

PARTS 12.1 and 12.2: Illicit Drug Use and the Proceeds of Crime   43

PART 13: Attempts and Conspiracies   45

PART 14: Jurisdiction   47

PART 15: Special Powers   49

PARTS 16 and 17: Appearance, Release, and Language   53

PARTS 18, 19, and 19.1: Preliminary Inquiries, Trials without a Jury, and Nunavut   55

PART 20: Jury Trials   57

PART 21: Appeals   66

PARTS 22, 23, and 24: Attendance, Sentencing, and Dangerous Offenders   68

PARTS 25, 26, 27, and 28: Recognizances, Extraordinary Remedies, Summary Convictions, and Forms   74

CONCLUSION

INDEX

Foreword

by the former Chief Justice of British Columbia

I was pleased when my longtime friend Les Vandor, QC, asked me to write a foreword to the Legal Counsel series of books he has written answering the most often asked questions about the law. This is a project that needs a lot of attention, and I applaud every attempt to explain and clarify the law.

It is often said, incorrectly I believe, that the law is a mystery to most people. That is because everything we do not understand is a mystery to us. The law can be very straightforward, as in the formation of a contract or the definition of negligence, or exceedingly difficult, as in the defence of insanity in a criminal law context or the interpretation of some sections of the Income Tax Act. What makes the difference, of course, is information.

Thus, the most junior lawyer knows that a contract is formed when an offer is accepted; that negligence is doing what a reasonable person would not do or not doing what a reasonable person would do; that the defence of insanity is more difficult and that even lawyers need to look at the most recent decision of the Supreme Court of Canada, *R.*

v. Stone, to understand this particular defence; and, as some lawyers say, that only God knows what some sections of the Income Tax Act mean.

So those who wonder about a legal question are searching for information that will help them to answer their questions or to understand that the complexities of some laws — usually dictated by the complexities of society — require much study and research before some questions can be answered.

What is often not understood is that when persons disagree about any matter, legal or otherwise, they are probably operating from different databases. I often think that, if only the public knew what I know about a case, it would agree with my decisions much more readily than is sometimes the case and vice versa in some cases. So it is important for the judiciary and the legal profession to provide information to the public so that it can more readily understand why the law is the way it is and why cases are decided the way they are.

Great strides have been made recently in this direction. Most courts now publish all their decisions on the Internet. Some authors are writing books about the law in engaging and understandable terms. I have tried to explain the judiciary and the criminal law in a legal compendium I have published on the Internet, and Les Vandor has tried to make the law more understandable through the medium of his radio show.

He has now gone one step further in agreeing to write

four books about the law. I am happy to have this opportunity to congratulate him for his energy and industry. I am confident that his endeavours will add greatly to public understanding of the law.

The Hon. Allan McEachern
former Chief Justice of British Columbia

Foreword

by the former Chief Justice of Nova Scotia

This book deals with many of the problems that confront and confound all of us in our daily lives whether it be on a personal, family, or business level.

Owning a home is the goal of most Canadian families. Acquiring a house appears to be a relatively simple proposition. But houses sit on land, and therein arise some of the most complex problems people face, especially if adequate investigation and care have not been taken before the contract to purchase is signed. Those who buy or rent a condominium or duplex, or apartment often wish, after the event, they were forewarned of pending pitfalls.

Consider the family cottage. Parents, convinced that there will never be dissension among their children, who "love the cottage," would be shocked after their demise to find that war has broken out among their offspring. On occasion, ownership and control of the beloved cottage become so fractured that it ends up being sold for the nonpayment of property taxes.

Unfortunately, many families are confronted with differences that lead to separation and divorce. Such circumstances are fraught with myriad difficult issues over who will own property and how the custody of children will be settled. It is much easier for judges to decide who should get Aunt Jessie's vase than how the children will be supported and by whom they will be raised.

None of us needs to establish a large company with its shares traded on a stock exchange to become involved in a corporate or commercial venture that can make us rich or do us in. Often a good idea is worth being patented or developed into a small business. Working with a friend or colleague may lead to the suggestion that a partnership be formed. The implications that result from totally innocent business associations can be devastating if plans are not properly documented.

The one thing that makes this book so useful is that in it Les Vandor, QC, has collected the real life experiences of Canadians. While it is not designed to be a legal text, it offers a practical guide to problems and their solutions.

For all of this, we owe Les Vandor our thanks.

The Hon. Lorne Clarke, OC, QC,
former Chief Justice of Nova Scotia

Preface

People write books for many reasons. Some write for money, while others have stories to tell. Some write to fill personal or social needs. I wrote as a result of a number of factors that seemed to coalesce at one time.

The first factor was a client who didn't pay me. I thought at the time that the advice I had given was good. Since I had done the research for the opinion, why not put the information I had gleaned from various sources to good use? I approached the CBC and suggested a call-in show on the topic I had researched. That was in 1992. Thus began for me a stint on radio giving free legal advice. I must thank the CBC (and in particular Dave Stephens and Elizabeth Hay) and its many listeners, whose questions are in this book.

The second factor was a neighbour who lived up the street. We have a variety of people who live nearby. We have economists, physicians, businesspeople, consultants, and military personnel. We have street parties. At a recent party, a neighbour in the book-publishing business suggested I write a book. I said maybe since he was the host and I was a polite guest. Were we under the influence of good cheer, or was this a serious option? I'd get back to him.

The third factor was a propensity to write. I scribbled on various pieces of paper and was fortunate to have had two pieces published in the *Globe and Mail*. I had always dreamed of writing a book of short stories. Law was not on the list. Yet law afforded me the opportunity to write.

In the weeks that followed, I was preoccupied with my ailing father. In the hospital, I engaged in small talk. I suggested a book, and my father said yes. I went home and began to write.

My aim in writing was to increase the public's basic understanding of the law. I didn't need to write just to see my name in print. My clients gave me that in some of the high-profile cases I had the honour of handling. These cases ranged from suing a TV station (the media loved that one) to fighting Revenue Canada (the public loved that one). I hope I have met the goal of public education.

I would like to thank my late father and Robert Ferguson (my neighbour). My wife and children took this project in stride, what with all the other crazy things I do. I thank my assistant, Robyn-Erin, for retyping various drafts and reminding me of some of the clients who walked in off the street. Without them, there would be no book. Let me also thank Dallas Harrison, my editor, who fixed my sentence structure. I wish that I could use his talents in my legal drafting. Thank you to all.

Introduction

The law is not a big, scary, incomprehensible beast. Dick the Butcher (an associate of Jack Cade), not Shakespeare, would have killed all lawyers, but lawyers and the law are part of our society, where rules and regulations govern our daily lives.

In primitive societies, the leader of a group or tribal chief would make decisions on a daily basis to settle disputes and set priorities. As a society evolved, the lord of the manor, and ultimately the king or queen, would establish rules and regulations for the orderly conduct of daily affairs. When problems arose, he or she would render a decision. Often the aggrieved persons would be so emotionally caught up with the problem that they would have a friend or family member assist them in advancing their cases. Thus began the idea of advocacy and ultimately a separate profession of lawyers.

While there may be good and bad lawyers, just like there are good and bad plumbers, a lawyer can assist not only in advocating your interests but also in protecting your rights. A classic example is your last will, in which you determine how to distribute your worldly goods after death. A lawyer can assist you in drafting the appropriate document.

Criticisms of lawyers often centre on the use of archaic terms. The use of legal terms is slowly giving way to plain language, as evidenced by insurance contracts that have become more and more readable. This is a direct result of the public's demand for straightforward language. The more the public demands this simple language, the more the legal profession will adopt it, if only for self-preservation.

In Canada, the system of justice is administered by federally and provincially appointed judges in every province and territory. It is no longer the case that the king or queen alone can dispense justice, given the size and complexity of our society. There are over 1,000 federally appointed judges who have the mandate of interpreting the laws passed by Parliament. They also settle individual disputes as they come before the courts.

Most provinces and territories have an entry-level court, often called a superior court. The superior court handles most disputes. If the parties are not satisfied with the result, there are provincial appeal courts that review and, if necessary, reverse the lower court's decision. The ultimate appeal court is the Supreme Court of Canada, which hears appeals from the provinces in both civil and criminal matters.

Judges are often criticized for making erroneous decisions or creating new laws, a domain traditionally reserved for Parliament. It is often suggested that those decisions are direct results of the input made by clients and their lawyers. If a client fails to tell a lawyer the full story, then the results can often be skewed. Similarly, if a lawyer fails to fully advance all relevant legal arguments, then a court cannot be blamed for rendering a decision that may not cover all issues. As a result, it is vital that individuals fully disclose their problems to their solicitors. To encourage full disclosure, the concept of solicitor-client privilege, similar to the privilege between a priest and a penitent, has been developed. The information given to a lawyer remains confidential and fully protected by law. In this fashion, a lawyer can be armed with all the relevant facts and protect or advance a client's interests to the fullest.

The fear often expressed by clients is that, if they tell the full story, a lawyer may refuse to take the case. A lawyer, and ultimately a court, must be armed with all the facts to properly solve a legal problem. Full disclosure is essential to this process and must be encouraged.

Criticism has been levied against lawyers for taking too much time explaining the law in a particular case. What I hope to do with this book is offer basic information on various areas of the law and provide answers to the most frequently asked questions. I hope that the book will assist readers in demystifying the law and understanding its basic concepts.

The questions that follow have been frequently asked by clients and CBC Radio listeners. Each section explains a legal concept, followed by the basic questions and answers in each area. You will also see inserts that provide further explanations, legal trivia, or stories to illustrate points. I also hope to debunk a few legal myths.

There are now four books in the series. What I hope to do in book one is explain the legal system and individual rights. In book two, I will cover issues surrounding the family and buying a home. In book three, I will cover retirement and estate planning and in book four, the criminal law. In this way, I will cover an individual's life, at least from a legal point of view, from birth to death and hopefully prevent you from getting into criminal trouble.

Remember, every case is different, and every new fact puts a wrinkle in the case. Provincial laws vary and often change. This book should be used as a guide and not necessarily the definitive solution to each situation. Yet basic principles can be explained and are applicable in many day-to-day situations.

Introduction to the Criminal Code

The Criminal Code of Canada has over 800 sections, each one with subsections and further subsections. Section 1 says that we can call the law "the Criminal Code." One of the last sections, Section 840, says that the government can add more provisions to the code. So the Criminal Code of Canada is an evolving concept, especially when we add cases from our courts that interpret and add to the law. Over the years, special laws have also been passed that graft more laws or conditions onto the Criminal Code. So, for example, when we talk about the powers of search and seizure, we may have to consider DNA sampling, in which case the DNA Identification Act kicks in.

The code has 28 parts. When the current code was first enacted in 1955, there was some semblance of logic, starting with crimes against society and followed by crimes against the person. Over the years, though, there have been many amendments, and legislators have often had to decide where to insert particular changes. As a result, some subsections have been added in the right places, while others have been inserted according to convenience rather than logic. For better or worse, I will follow the order of the code and try to tie various sections together.

In this volume, I will summarize the law in its basic format. Since a book of this nature cannot cover all the sections of the Criminal Code, I will focus on what I believe are its main provisions. Now and then, I will meander to discuss trivial laws such as the criminal laws governing oysters and wizards such as Harry Potter.

I have the usual word of caution. Some areas of law are quite technical, and some laws can severely affect your liberty. So, while you can take on a Small Claims Court action over a defective DVD, you'd be wise to hire a lawyer if you're facing a murder charge. Also remember that the code interacts with many other laws and regulations. No one provision can be read on its own.

Part 1: The General Rules

The Criminal Code starts with some general rules. Section 6 says that you are presumed innocent until proven guilty. This is a fundamental provision of our law. Section 7, previously of little concern, covers acts committed by Canadians while on an aircraft. If you break the law while on an aircraft flying over international waters, the code deems your actions to have been committed in Canada, so our laws apply. An example of amendments added to an existing section, Section 7 also covers acts committed by Canadians while on oil rigs moored on the continental shelf or while in a space station. As a Canadian, you are subject to Canadian law whether you are out at sea or out in space.

Section 13 says that no person under the age of 12 can be convicted, as child protection laws kick in, while Section 14 says that you can't consent to being killed. The latter section covers assisted suicide and was the subject of a major challenge before the Supreme Court of Canada.

Ignorance of the law is considered no excuse, and that principle is covered in Section 19. Sections 21 to 24 cover parties to an offence, so that, if one person robs a convenience store and his or her accomplice drives the getaway car, both can be convicted of robbery. In Sections 25 to 33, police are given the power to arrest and to use force if necessary.

In Section 34, self-defence is allowed if you are the

subject of an unprovoked attack, but self-inflicted intoxication, when you have no sense of what you are doing, is not a defence to a charge under the Criminal Code. The use of reasonable force against children ("spanking") is allowed under Section 43, and that provision was recently ruled to be constitutional.

Apart from some definitions, such as what constitutes sexual intercourse ("penetration to even the slightest degree, notwithstanding that seed is not emitted"), that is the first part and the foundation of the Criminal Code.

Q: Do I have to say anything to the police when they interview me?

A: Yes; otherwise, you may be obstructing an investigation.

Q: Do the police have an obligation to warn me that anything I say may be used to charge me?

A: Not until you're a suspect.

In April of 2001 the Dutch Government enacted a law to legalize **euthanasia** and assisted suicides. In May of 2001 an Australian entrepreneur announced that he would launch a ship to offer mercy killings and burials at sea outside of any country's national jurisdiction. The well-known U.S. physician Jack Kevorkian was recently jailed for assisting in a suicide. In Canada under our Criminal Code, it's illegal to counsel, aid, or abet a person to commit suicide, whether suicide ensues or not. In addition, the victim's consent does not absolve you from the offence. Even a Power of Attorney for Medical Care won't absolve you from liability. The only option for those wanting a change appears to be a change in the law.

Q: Can I use force to stop my neighbour from driving over my property?

A: You are allowed to fence your property, and you are allowed to post signs stating that it is private property. However, if a neighbour refuses to respect your property, you should give him or her ample warning that you intend to take appropriate measures. They include calling the police and using reasonable force to protect your property.

Q: I've heard of children being sent to adult court. What does that mean?

A: Our criminal laws apply to children over 12 years of age. For children over 12, the Young Offenders Act — one of those laws grafted onto the Criminal Code — kicks in. Separate sentencing options are available if you're over 12 but under 18. If the accused is within that range but the offence is serious, Crown lawyers can ask a judge to take up the case in a higher court. This higher court is often called adult court since the accused persons there are all adults. If the accused is under 12, he or she is dealt with by provincial child welfare laws and may be sent to a group home or a specialized care facility.

When is an offence a crime? The answer was set out over 75 years ago.

FROM THE SUPREME COURT OF CANADA IN THE CASE OF THE KING vs. BELL (1925) S.C.R. 59

[When the relevant law] imposed a duty in the public interest; that default in performing that duty constituted an offence against the public law; and that Parliament provided for the infliction of a prescribed punishment by a tribunal which ordinarily exercises criminal jurisdiction and by procedure enacted by the Criminal Code.

Part 2: Offences against Public Order

When the criminal law was first developed, it focused on offences against the Crown or the country at large. These laws still exist. We still have the crime of high treason in Section 46. A Canadian commits high treason if, among other things, he or she kills or attempts to kill the ruling monarch, does the monarch bodily harm, engages in war against Canada, or assists an enemy at war with Canada. Assisting an enemy includes helping that enemy when Canadian forces are in its territory.

After the attack on the World Trade Center on September 11, 2001, President George W. Bush of the United States of America declared war on terrorism. Canada joined the United States in fighting terrorism and sent troops to Afghanistan, the declared war zone. Under Section 46 of the Criminal Code, anyone assisting the "enemy" in Afghanistan would be guilty of high treason. The punishment? Life in a Canadian prison.

Sabotage (impairing the efficiency of a working vessel, vehicle, or aircraft) is covered by Section 52 and does not cover repairs to your car. Mutiny (inciting members of the Canadian Forces to be traitors) is covered in Section 53, while piracy (stealing a Canadian ship or cargo) is dealt with in Section 74. Duelling is illegal under Section 71, and you are subject to two years of imprisonment if convicted. Prize fighting without boxing gloves of no less than 140 grams is illegal under Section 83, unless an athletic board or commission set up by a province regulates the activity.

Section 83 underscores the interesting interplay of federal and provincial governments. Under the **Constitution**, the criminal law is set by the federal government. Provincial governments can also pass some criminal-type laws and at times regulate activities to make them legal. For example, if you have a car accident and leave the scene without reporting the accident, you can be convicted of the criminal offence of failing to remain at the scene of a crime. Yet the same offence can be covered by a provincial highway traffic act. The difference is not so much in the penalty as in having a criminal record if you are convicted under the Criminal Code. Similarly, prize fighting can be provincially regulated and allowed to take place.

FROM THE ONTARIO HIGH COURT IN THE CASE OF REGINA vs. RACIMORE JULY 7, 1975

". . . there is no mistake and no misunderstanding of the essential fact that an accident had occurred. In the present case there was no knowledge of contact and the accused was therefore ignorant of the existence of an accident when he drove his vehicle away and failed to remain at the scene. His failure to remain was dictated by . . . ignorance . . ."

Should you be charged with high treason, this is how the charge would be read out in court: "John Q. Doe on the 1st day of January 2005 at 00:01 hours in This Town, Canada, did attempt to kill Her Majesty and did thereby commit high treason, contrary to Section 47(1) of the Criminal Code of Canada." Should you be charged with mutiny, this is how that charge would be read out: "John Q. Doe on the 1st day of January 2005 at 00:01 hours in This Town did attempt to seduce for a traitorous purpose Captain Jane Q. Public, a member of the Canadian Forces, from her duty and allegiance to Her Majesty, to wit by demanding the keys to HMCS *Our Ship*, contrary to Section 53(a) of the Criminal Code of Canada."

Q: A family member was involved in an automobile accident and charged with "following too closely." Can the prosecution successfully press the charge when the police officer charged him only on the basis that he ran into the back of the other vehicle — that is, the officer didn't observe the distance between the vehicles before they collided? Does the officer have to inform a person involved in an accident that the report he is asked to give may result in a charge — that is, do we have the right to remain silent when questioned after an accident?

A: It is standard procedure in rear-end collisions to charge the rear-most driver with following too closely. Unless you can prove that the car ahead suddenly and without warning (say defective taillights) stopped, the charge will "stick." As for the right to remain silent, unfortunately much of that notion comes from TV. When you are formally charged, you have the right to counsel and silence, but the officer is fully within his or her right to ask about the accident without the warning.

Q: I have a criminal record but want to get rid of it. Can I?

A: If you've served your time, you can ask for a pardon, which, if granted, wipes the slate clean. Not every person will qualify, but if you've been convicted of a minor offence there should be no problem in getting a pardon.

Q: The police have dropped all charges against me, but I was fingerprinted. Can I have that record destroyed?

A: Yes. You or your lawyer can ask for that record to be destroyed. All you have to do is write to the police officer in charge of your case and ask.

Kiss Me

Late one Friday afternoon, I received a call from a young man facing a court hearing the following Monday. The charge was reckless driving. He was concerned and thought that he might need a lawyer.

According to the charge, he'd been driving north on a prominent Toronto street. An officer had observed him slightly swerving out of and back into his lane. There had been one other passenger in the car: his new fiancée. He had just proposed to her, and in the ensuing excitement she had leaned over and kissed him on the cheek. The kiss had caused him to swerve.

On the witness stand, I proceeded to ask questions about the kiss. Was it a peck or a French kiss? Was there saliva involved? The ensuing reaction from the judge and the audience was predictable: there were chuckles throughout the courtroom. The charge was dismissed, and in the space of Friday to Monday the file was closed.

Q: I was arrested after leaving a bar and getting into an accident. During the arrest, I was roughly handled and pushed into the cop car. I blame one of the arresting officers for my subsequent memory loss. Can I sue the police?

A: You have six months from the time of the incident to complain and sue the police. You should thoroughly investigate the matter and obtain independent witnesses if possible.

Q: I was accused of shoplifting a small bag of cookies. The store's video camera proved that I was innocent. Can I sue the store?

A: Yes, especially since you were wrongly accused and the police have not pressed charges. I would write to the manager of the store to ask for an apology; if you don't get one, you can consider suing the store for damage to your reputation.

Many Criminal cases require funding from **Legal Aid** plans as people just can't afford a lawyer or the cost of a trial. Unfortunately many of these plans are running out of money and many a plan, in an effort to save money, has set the threshold for qualifying quite high. In some provinces you will only qualify for Legal Aid if you make below $12,000 per year, which in itself is bare subsistence living. If you make more, you won't qualify for aid. Recently lawyers in many provinces have gone on strike in support of more funding for their clients.

Part 3: Firearms

The possession and use of firearms or other weapons have led to much debate and legislation. There are laws governing firearms in the Criminal Code, and there are separate rules on licensing and registration of firearms. Simply put, you can't own a gun in Canada unless you hold a valid licence. While in the United States there is a constitutional right to bear arms, Canada has taken a different approach in regulating their use. Charlton Heston, a well-known U.S. actor and gun lobbyist, found little favour in Canada when he spoke against current Canadian laws.

Like all the other sections of the Criminal Code, the firearm section starts with definitions, and it defines for exclusion from regulation guns manufactured before 1898. Prohibited weapons include guns whose barrels are "equal to or less than 105 mm in length." Yet provincial sporting organizations can allow for the use of longer or shorter guns. Also, devices used in emergencies, such as flare guns, or devices used for slaughtering animals are not considered firearms in the code. In an odd twist, an individual recently registered a power tool as a firearm.

The use of a gun as well as a particular offence can form the basis of a separate charge as set out in Section 85. As with many provisions, the penalty is set out. The reason is simple: when the government outlawed **the death penalty**, the trade-off was to set out various penalties in the code. Hence, for many offences, the code stipulates the exact penalty. For improper use of a gun, it's between one and fourteen years for a first offence; for a second offence, it's between three and fourteen years.

Now, when people are convicted of an offence, you often hear that they have been sentenced to serve concurrent sentences. Depending on the particular crime, a person can be charged with multiple offences, such as robbery and the use of a gun. If the person is convicted of both offences, the code provides separate penalties. Does the person then serve the sentences concurrently or separately? If the penalty for robbery is one year, and that for the use of a gun is also one year, does the person serve a total of two years in jail or one year for both offences, serving the sentences concurrently? In this example, the answer lies in Section 85 of the code: the sentences must be served one after the other. The idea is to stiffen the penalty if a weapon is used. In other cases, the judge can order that the sentences be served at the same time.

You can't point a loaded or unloaded weapon at someone (Section 87), and you can't carry a concealed weapon on your person (Section 90) or in a car (Section 94). You can't alter a gun to make it automatic (Section 102), and you can import or export a weapon only with a special licence (Section 103). If you lose a gun, it's an offence not to tell the police (Section 105). If convicted of a weapons offence, you will be prohibited from possessing a weapon for the duration of your sentence (Section 109).

The code has some fairly new provisions allowing for search and seizure. The general rule is that, when the police want to search your home or office, they need to appear before a judge or justice of the peace and obtain a search warrant. A **search warrant** is nothing more than a court order allowing the police to enter your property. In the case of firearms, if the police believe that you may possess prohibited weapons, under Section 117.02 they can conduct a search without a warrant.

Again, the general rule is that you are presumed innocent, and it's up to the police and the lawyers prosecuting you to prove their case. This is called the **onus of proof**. For many of the weapons offences in the code, this onus is shifted to the accused person. Section 117.11, which has been added to the code, requires the accused to prove that he or she holds a valid licence or is duly authorized to carry a firearm or weapon.

Q: I have a Second World War rifle. Do I have to do anything given new firearm laws?

A: In both the Criminal Code and separate legislation, there are laws governing firearms. Under the law, you have to register all firearms or surrender them to the police for destruction. If your rifle has some historical value, however, you can consider donating it to a museum. A donation would comply with the law.

A **handgun** is defined quite broadly as: "a firearm that is designed, altered or intended to be aimed and fired by the action of one hand, whether or not it has been redesigned or subsequently altered to be aimed and fired by the action of both hands."

Q: Can the government regulate my owning a gun?

A: Yes. Since the government has been duly elected and the Charter of Rights and Freedoms allows reasonable restrictions on individual rights for the benefit of society at large, the gun laws are valid.

Privilege

If a client walks in and places a gun on a lawyer's desk, stating that the gun was used in a murder, does the lawyer have to tell the police?

This ethical dilemma has been debated for years in law schools and societies. In theory, a lawyer isn't required to help the police prove their case against the client. On the other hand, the lawyer has evidence of a murder and may, under certain circumstances, be considered an accomplice.

One view is for the lawyer to try to negotiate the best possible deal for the client while disclosing the evidence during privileged negotiations. The other view is for the lawyer to take the matter to trial but not to call evidence that would harm the case. A proposed alternative is to have a committee of peers provide an answer in that particular case.

Part 4: Offences against the Administration of Justice

This part of the Criminal Code outlaws bribery of judicial and other law enforcement officials such as police officers, and fraud or breach of trust by municipal officials. Making misleading statements in court — that is, lying — is called perjury and is covered in Section 131.

Perjury is the *intentional* misleading of a court or judicial official. The concept of intention is key to criminal law in Canada. Whenever an offence is committed, two elements are at play. The first is the act itself, in Latin the **actus reus**. The second is the intention to commit the act, in Latin the **mens rea**. To be convicted, both elements have to be present. So, if you are accused of leaving the scene of a crime, you have a defence if you didn't know that a crime or even the event itself had occurred. Although ignorance of the law is no excuse, you have to commit a crime intentionally to be convicted of it. The reasoning goes back to the belief that people are able to choose right from wrong, so, if they choose wrong intentionally, mens rea is present.

Section 144 gives prisoners a further and maximum ten-year sentence if they try to escape and a further two years if they succeed but are later caught. And a jailor who helps a convict to escape can be sentenced to two years in jail. If you help a prisoner of war escape, you could face five years in jail.

Q: (The CBC broadcasts into Canadian penitentiaries. During this call, you could hear the caller's fellow inmates cheering him on.) The warden won't let me out of jail. How can I get out of jail?

A: When you're sent to jail, the presiding judge will sign an order for incarceration. You are often given a copy of that order, or you can get a copy from either your lawyer or the courthouse where you were sentenced. If the court order confirms that you have served your time, you should send a copy to the warden, and hopefully you'll be let out of jail.

On December 10, 2001 the Ontario Court of Appeal dealt with a lawsuit by a German/Canadian businessman against the Governments of Canada and Germany. The Plaintiff claimed damages for abuse of power arguing that he was improperly arrested and detained in connection with an **extradition** request. A lower court had stopped the damage claim against Germany only. The matter ended up in the Supreme Court of Canada (SCC) with Amnesty International intervening on behalf of the Plaintiff/businessman. Amnesty argued in a legal brief that individuals should be able to sue governments over physical or mental abuse by the State. In separate rulings, the SCC allowed the suit against Canada but not against Germany.

Q: What is extradition?

A: Canada has signed treaties with many countries. Some of these treaties cover the criminal law. The idea is that, if a Canadian commits a criminal offence and flees to another country, that individual will be returned to Canada to face trial. Similarly, if a foreigner flees to Canada, he or she will be sent back home. The only new wrinkle is extradition to a country where the death penalty remains part of the law. Canada will not extradite an accused person if he or she may face the death penalty if tried in the home country.

Maxwell Smart Redux

As a young law student working in Quebec after the October Crisis in 1970, I was asked to go out one summer's day and have an affidavit signed. An affidavit is a sworn statement about certain events. The person signing the affidavit, the affiant, happened to be in a minimum-security prison just north of Montreal. This was my first visit to a jail.

I drove up to what I thought was the main entrance. I entered, told the guard my purpose, and was searched. As it turned out, I was in the wrong building, but the guard told me how to get to the right cell block. So I got back into my car, drove to the appropriate entrance, and was ushered in without a further search.

Anyone who has watched the TV series *Get Smart* will recall the opening sequence, in which agent Maxwell Smart walks down a hall. As he passes doorway after doorway, the metal doors slam shut. It was exactly like this at this facility as I walked down the hall.

At the end of the hall was a room. There were two doors, a table, and two chairs. I entered by one of those doors and sat down. After a long time, the other door opened, and in walked the affiant. He shook my hand. It was then that I realized he had no fingers. He'd lost them in an October Crisis bomb blast.

I began to sweat as I explained my purpose, but he was friendly, and he signed on the dotted line. It was over in a matter of minutes. I felt relieved.

As I stood up, I heard the words "Sit down." Was I to be a hostage? Just as the movie of my life began flashing in my brain (the opening credits having just finished), the affiant explained that, because of the two-door system, he had to leave first, and then I'd be let out. You can well imagine how fast my feet carried me to my car.

Part 5: Sexual Offences

As you might expect, the law governs every aspect of your life, including sex. According to Section 150.1, it is illegal to have sex with a person under the age of 14, even if that person consents. It's not a defence to say that you believed the person was over 14 at the time. Even touching, for sexual purposes, a person younger than 14 is an offence under Section 151 and is subject to 10 years in jail.

Incest — having sex with a parent, child, brother, or sister — is punishable under Section 155 by 14 years in jail. Anal intercourse is punishable by 10 years in jail except if done in private and consented to by adults over 18 years of age. If the act is done with more than two people present, it's deemed not to be private and is an offence.

Making or possessing obscene materials is an offence under Section 163. A crime comic that depicts the commission of a real or fake crime is also outlawed. Similarly, child pornography is outlawed in Section 163.1. Immoral theatrical performances are covered in Section 167.

Section 173 punishes indecent acts committed in a public place, and Section 174 makes it illegal to be nude in a public place, subject to the activity being regulated by local authorities such as municipal swimming pools.

While this part of the code covers sexual activity and public nuisances, Section 176 is included as well. According to this section, it is an offence to disturb the clergy going to or from their place of work, a holdover from the days of unpopular sermons and public riots that may have occurred as a result of what was said during a particular service. Interestingly, Section 181 makes it an offence to spread false news. This part of the code ends with Section 182, which makes it an offence to neglect or interfere with a dead body.

Sexual interference is a defined term. "Every person who, for a sexual purpose, touches, directly or indirectly, with a part of the body or with an object, any part of the body of a person under the age of fourteen years is guilty . . . and is liable to imprisonment for a term not exceeding ten years . . ."

Q: Can one person argue that he or she thought the other person was of legal age when they had sex?

A: No. The law is clear, and even consent to sex is not a defence if the person is under 14.

The Age-Old Question

In Alberta, Saskatchewan, Manitoba, Ontario, Quebec, and Prince Edward Island, the age of majority (i.e., you are considered an adult and can do most everything) is 18. Everywhere else in Canada, it is 19. Yet you can vote in a federal election once you're 18.

In Ontario, you can drive, leave home or school permanently, work full time, or get married at age 16. You can also serve liquor when you're 18 but can drink it only when you're 19.

Part 6: Privacy

The right to privacy is often subject to the needs of society. In England, where people have lived with terrorism for a long time, public video cameras are the norm, and people have come to accept that invasion of their privacy. In Canada, however, we are still debating how much of our privacy we wish to give up.

Section 184 of the Criminal Code dispels a common myth: you can't record the conversation of another person without his or her permission. The exception is when it's done by the police when they investigate crimes or by a telephone company in servicing the phone lines. The code sets out details on how and when police can obtain a wiretap and the role of a judge in reviewing an application for a wiretap.

When criminal matters are brought to court, lawyers acting for the Crown have to prove the case against an accused person. This is called the **burden of proof**. For criminal matters, to get a conviction, they have to prove the case beyond a **reasonable doubt**. This is in contrast to civil or commercial matters, where to win you have to prove your case on a **balance of probabilities** — that is, your version of events is likely the correct one.

So, if it's clear that A killed B, he or she must be acquitted of murder if the killing might have been accidental, because, in that case, the matter has not been proven beyond a reasonable doubt. (The Supreme Court of Canada plans to elaborate on this in an upcoming case.)

> "Every one who, by means of any electro-magnetic, acoustic, mechanical or other device, **willfully intercepts** a private communication is guilty . . . and liable to imprisonment for a term not exceeding five years."

Q: Can my neighbour videotape my comings and goings?

A: No, since you have the right to privacy and since the Supreme Court has recently said (to paraphrase) that you can't take a picture of someone without his or her consent unless the person is part of a crowd.

Q: If I tape someone's phone call, can I use it in a civil lawsuit?

A: No. It's illegal to tape another person's conversation without that person's permission. Unless you have such permission, orally or in writing, you can't use the tape.

Q: What if someone wears a police "wire"? Can I be taped?

A: Yes. If a police informant or officer wears a "wire" (i.e., a microphone and/or taping device), it's generally assumed that the police have either a judge's order or reasonable and probable grounds to conduct the taping.

Part 7: Gaming and Prostitution

This section of the Criminal Code begins by covering gaming and betting. Originally, these provisions of law were meant to prevent cheating and outlaw gambling. Since lotteries and the like generate revenue for governments, the law now focuses on regulating gaming. So, while owning a slot machine is in itself illegal (Section 198), you are allowed to own or use one as part of a social club, if the machine is licensed by a province, or if it has been adapted to dispense free games only.

Section 202 makes it illegal to bet, so, if you flip a coin in the office to determine who buys coffee, you have technically committed a criminal offence and can be sent to jail, for a first offence, for up to two years. The card game called Three-Card Monte is outlawed in Section

206, though the game itself is not defined or explained. (Anyone who knows how to play should tell me, but if you show me how it will be a criminal offence!)

Lotteries are regulated in Section 207, and houses of "ill repute" or "bawdy houses" are outlawed in Section 210. In addition to outlawing prostitution, Section 213 focuses on sex and cars. Any person who stops a car, impedes the flow of traffic, or tries to speak to another person in a car for the purpose of having sex is guilty of an offence under the law.

A **slot machine** is defined in Section 198 as any machine:

(a) that is used or intended to be used for any purpose other than vending merchandise or services, or

(b) that is used or intended to be used for the purpose of vending merchandise or services if

   (i) the result of one or any number of operations of the machine is a matter of chance or uncertainty to the operator,

   (ii) as a result of a given number of successive operations by the operator the machine produces different results, or

   (iii) on any operation of the machine it discharges or emits a slug or token

but does not include an automatic machine or slot machine that dispenses as prizes only one or more free games on that machine.

Q: Does my church need a licence for a games night?

A: Yes, since most forms of gaming are outlawed or at least regulated. Provincial authorities should be contacted about obtaining a licence.

Q: What if I own a slot machine and give away free games? Is that legal?

A: The Criminal Code allows the use of slot machines if the only prize is another free game. Yet the machine must be regulated by the province, and it can't be used to lure people into other illegal activities.

"John School"

As an alternative to serving time in jail, people caught with prostitutes can go to a special school called "John school." They learn about the effects of prostitution on women, men, and society in general. After attending these classes, the person caught with a prostitute receives no criminal record. Not everyone qualifies for this school, and it depends on negotiations between your lawyer and the Crown as well as on your background.

Part 8: Offences against the Person

Part 8 of the Criminal Code begins by protecting the sanctity of life. This follows the laws on protecting the state.

Section 215 requires parents or guardians to provide the necessities of life to anyone under the age of 16. The law presumes that a duty exists if you provide this care to a child even if it's not your legitimate child. A one-month lapse is sufficient ground for laying a charge. The code then deals in Sections 219 to 240 with murder. Various terms are defined.

1. **Criminal negligence** causing death occurs when you have a wanton disregard for the safety of another person who dies as a result of your actions.
2. **Homicide**, a general term, occurs when you cause the death of another human being. Homicide can be culpable (deserving blame) or non culpable. Culpable homicide occurs when you cause the death of another person by an unlawful act or, for example, by wilfully frightening to death a child or sick person. If you injure a child before or during birth, and the child subsequently dies, this is also considered homicide.
3. If it's culpable homicide, it then gets slotted into either murder or manslaughter or infanticide.
   a. Culpable homicide is called **murder** when you mean to cause someone to die. It can be classified as first- or second-degree murder. First-degree murder is when it's planned and deliberate. Several

cases automatically get slotted into first-degree murder, such as killing a police officer. Most other murders can be slotted into or considered second-degree murder.

b. Culpable homicide is called **manslaughter** if death occurred in the heat of violence caused by sudden provocation.

c. Culpable homicide is called **infanticide** if a woman kills her newborn child.

The penalties on conviction vary. For first- and second-degree murder and manslaughter, it's life in prison. For infanticide, it can be up to five years in jail.

Section 241 makes it illegal to aid anyone in committing suicide. The code then deals, as in the section on sex, with motor vehicles. Section 249 deals with the dangerous operation of a car, while Section 252 deals with failing to stop or remain at the scene of an accident. A similar offence exists in most provincial highway laws, the difference being that with the code you get a criminal record.

Sections 254 and following allow for breath or blood testing if you drive while under the influence of alcohol.

You can be sent to jail for five years under Section 264.1 of the code if you threaten to cause harm to a person, her property, or her pet. If you attempt to or do apply force to a person, it is called "assault" (Section 265), and you can also be sent to jail for five years. The law applies to all forms of assault, including sexual assault.

Kidnapping, hostage taking, and abduction are covered in Sections 279 to 286 and include removing a child from the custody of a spouse. Abortions are now regulated by Section 287 of the code. Bigamy and polygamy (having more than one spouse) are outlawed under Sections 290 and 293. And although there are civil remedies for libel and slander, the code covers libel in Section 297 and following. In other words, you can be both civilly and criminally liable if you defame someone, especially if it's considered hate propaganda.

Q: What is a life sentence?

A: A life sentence is exactly that, a sentence in jail for life. Depending on the crime, an individual may be eligible for parole after, say, 25 years, unless the judge in sentencing has put restrictions on parole.

Q: Someone is constantly telling people that I am a thief. I'm innocent. What can I do?

A: When someone makes a statement about you that is untrue, you have the right to an apology and the right to sue for damages to your reputation. Damages may include lost income or opportunity caused by the false statement. If it is serious enough, the police may well get involved. Your first step is to get witnesses to support your version of events. You should then write a polite letter asking for an apology. If you get a letter of apology in return, you should send it on to whoever heard the false accusation. If you don't get an apology, consider dropping the matter or, as a last resort, suing the person.

**FROM THE SUPREME COURT OF CANADA
IN THE CASE OF RODRIGUEZ vs.
THE ATTORNEY GENERAL OF CANADA ET AL.
SEPTEMBER 30, 1993**

The appellant, a 42-year-old mother, suffers from amyotrophic lateral sclerosis. Her condition is rapidly deteriorating and she will soon lose the ability to swallow, speak, walk, and move her body without assistance. Thereafter she will lose the capacity to breathe without a respirator, to eat without a gastrotomy and will eventually become confined to bed. Her life expectance is between 2 and 14 months. The appellant does not wish to die so long as she still has the capacity to enjoy life, but wishes that a qualified physician be allowed to set up technological means by which she might, when she is no longer able to enjoy life, by her own hand, at the time of her choosing, end her life. The appellant applied to the Supreme Court of British Columbia for an order that s. 241(b) of the Criminal Code, which prohibits the giving of assistance to commit suicide, be declared invalid on the ground that it violates her rights under ss. 7, 12 and 15 of the Charter, and is therefore, to the extent it precludes a terminally ill person from committing "physician-assisted" suicide, of no force and effect by virtue of s. 52(1) of the Constitution Act, 1982. . . .

Assisted suicide, outlawed under the common law, has been prohibited by Parliament since the adoption of Canada's first Criminal Code. The long-standing blanket prohibition in s. 241(b), which fulfils the government's objective of protecting the vulnerable, is grounded in the state interest in protecting life and reflects the policy of the state that human life should not be deprecated by allowing life to be taken. This state policy is part of our fundamental conception of the sanctity of life. A blanket prohibition on assisted suicide similar to that in section 241(b) also seems the norm among Western democracies, and as such a prohibition has never been adjudged to be unconstitutional or contrary to fundamental human rights. These societies, including Canada, recognize and generally apply the principle of the sanctity of life subject to narrow exceptions where notions of personal autonomy and dignity must prevail. Distinctions between passive and active forms of intervention in the dying process continue to be drawn and assisted suicide in situations such as the appellant's is prohibited with few exceptions. No consensus can be found in favour of the decriminalization of assisted suicide. To the extent that there is a consensus, it is that human life must be respected. This consensus finds legal expression in our legal system which prohibits capital punishment. The prohibition against assisted suicide serves a similar purpose. Parliament's repeal of the offence of attempted suicide from the Criminal Code was not a recognition that suicide was to be accepted within Canadian society. Rather, this action merely reflected the recognition that the criminal law was an ineffectual and inappropriate tool for dealing with suicide attempts. Given the concern about abuse and the great difficulty in creating appropriate safeguards, the blanket prohibition an assisted suicide is not arbitrary or unfair. The prohibition relates to the state's interest in protecting the vulnerable and is reflective of fundamental values at play in our society. Section 241(b) therefore does not infringe s. 7 of the Charter.

Q: I'm divorced. Do I have to support my child after age 16?

A: It depends on your separation and divorce agreement. Generally, you have to support a child during his or her full-time education, up to the age of 25. The Criminal Code governs situations in which you neglect your child or fail to provide basic necessities.

Q: Can I sue someone for damaging my name and reputation?

A: Yes, and such damage is called defamation. If your reputation is hurt by printed words, it's called "libel"; if your reputation is hurt by spoken words, it's called "slander." Both are subject to civil liabilities and remedies; they are also regulated by the Criminal Code.

Assault and Battery

To attempt to beat another person without touching him or her is **assault**. The beating of another that includes touching (however slight) in anger is **battery**. In common terms, the word *assault* is used to include *battery*.

Q: Why do charges sometimes get changed before a trial?

A: There can be many reasons why charges are changed. The police in conjunction with the Crown lawyers may decide that there is not enough evidence for a particular charge. They may have been given further information by the accused's lawyer that has changed their minds. Alternatively, an accused and his lawyer may agree to plead guilty to a lesser charge.

Q: What is plea bargaining?

A: Plea bargaining occurs when the lawyers for the accused and the Crown agree that the accused will plead guilty to a lesser charge as opposed to fighting a more serious charge.

Q: I am 30 years old and was abused in grade school. Can I bring the guilty people up on criminal charges?

A: Yes. It's never too late to raise issues of abuse. You should contact the local police or Crown lawyers with your story so that they can investigate and lay charges.

Part 9: Property

Theft is defined in Section 322 as depriving someone intentionally of his or her property. **Robbery** is theft with an element of violence or threat. If you take another person's oysters (not those on the dining plate), you have committed theft under Section 323. It's also illegal under Section 338 to steal cattle or deface a brand on cattle.

According to Section 339, it's illegal to take, hold, keep, conceal, receive, appropriate, remove, alter, or obliterate lumber found adrift in any river, stream, lake, harbour, or coastal water. The exception is if you're licensed as a beachcomber or work as an actor performing the task of a beachcomber.

By amendment, Section 342.1 makes it illegal to tap into computers ("hacking"). You can be sentenced to two years in jail, and a judge can order that your computer be forfeited to the government. If you charge in excess of 60% interest a year on an outstanding debt, you are charging a criminal interest rate under Section 347.

Breaking into someone's home (called a B and E) is covered in Section 348, possessing property obtained by theft is outlawed in Section 354, and stealing mail is covered in Section 356. If you pretend to practise witchcraft, you have committed a criminal act under Section 365. So, when your kids dress up like Harry Potter and pretend to be witches or wizards, they have technically committed an offence, although it's unlikely that any police officer would enforce that section of the code. If you are a witch and can prove it in a court of law, you have committed no offence — the code covers pretending only.

This section of the code then ends with making it illegal to forge money or damage official registers, including election documents.

Q: During recent antigovernment protests, pretend money was handed out as a means of protesting government policy. Also, at Christmas time, some retailers sell fake million-dollar bills. Are these things legal?

A: You are allowed to protest government policies since protesting is part of free speech. But you can't forge currency or otherwise copy Canadian money. In laying charges, the police will consider whether anyone was misled by the fake money and whether it was printed just as a joke. As part of its advertising, a major newspaper chain uses the image of the queen as it appears on paper money. Since no one is being misled and it's only part of the currency, it's legal.

"Every one who commits **forgery**
(a) is guilty . . . and liable to imprisonment for a term not exceeding ten years . . ."

Part 10: Fraud

If you see a quarter lying on the ground, chances are you'll pick it up. That quarter used to belong to someone who has lost it. "Finders keepers" isn't really part of our law, yet you'll likely keep the quarter. Whether on the simple level of a quarter on the ground or on the complex level of the collapse of energy giant Enron, fraud happens, and everyone is involved at times. Former Prime Minister St. Laurent's grandson is a fraud buster in Florida. Who would have thought that a Canadian prime minister's grandson would live and work in the U.S. . . . then again, many have sent their own kids to American universities.

Part 10 of the Criminal Code deals with fraud. You can be sent to jail for up to 10 years if you defraud someone of her property or money. The definition of fraud is wide and includes giving someone a false receipt (Section 388). So, if you give a contractor $1,000 in cash, but he gives you a $1,500 receipt for tax purposes, both of you have committed an offence under the code. And, speaking of Enron, accused of issuing false financial information, Section 400 makes it an offence to raise money using false information.

Now here is a task for linguists. When a comedian goes on stage and pretends to be a major political figure, we call that "impersonation." Section 403 of the code makes it an offence to "personate" a person, living or dead, with the intention of gaining advantage. Is the proper word "personate" or the more popular "impersonate"? Is the comedian a criminal offender or just offensive?

Section 417 makes it illegal to sell defective goods to the government (a holdover from the First World War), and Section 419 makes it illegal to dress up like a member of the Canadian Forces unless you really are a member.

Uniforms

Now ponder this: in Ottawa, there is a rule, a holdover from the Cold War, that not all military personnel are allowed to wear military dress on public streets. The idea was that, if all personnel were to wear their uniforms, the enemy could calculate the number of personnel in Ottawa. By having some wear military uniforms and others dress in civilian clothes, we can fool the enemy. What military planners forgot was mathematical averaging, whereby you can calculate the number of personnel by averaging numbers on the street.

Q: I bought a membership in an American vacation club. I'm now being asked to kick in more money, and it looks like I won't be able to sell my membership. I think I've been taken. Is there anything I can do?

A: There are rules governing these vacation clubs. You should contact your provincial ministry of consumer and business relations. If you think you've been the victim of a fraud or scam, contact the police as well.

They may already have a file on the club, they may want to alert other potential investors, and they may work with American authorities.

Q: Can I be forced to take a lie detector test?

A: No, but a lie detector test (polygraph) may help to prove your innocence. It's one of many pieces of evidence that a court will consider.

Bambi

A former U.S. police officer, nicknamed Bambi, was accused of killing her husband and was arrested in Canada. She fought extradition on the basis that a key piece of evidence, a polygraph test, had been improperly conducted.

At the extradition hearing, expert witnesses were called to testify on the use and evidentiary weight of polygraphs in general. The Crown witness was asked if he had reviewed the legal literature on polygraphs. He said, "Yes, even the paper written by Vandor." Since this was a high-profile extradition case, many media people attended the trial. Within minutes, my phone began to ring. I was asked for copies of my paper.

> Unfortunately, the expert had failed to say that my "paper" was a brief report to the government of Canada and was covered by confidentiality rules. It could not be produced or released without government approval. The government refused to grant this approval, so all I could say was the trite phrase "No comment."

Parts 11 and 12: Forbidden Property Acts and Currency

Despite the fancy title, these brief parts cover mischief, arson, setting a false fire alarm, interfering with the rescue of a vessel in distress, and cruelty to animals. Why we group arson with vessels and animals is a mystery to me.

Cruelty to animals is an offence under our criminal laws. But what if you train a dog to attack, and it kills someone? That was exactly the situation in a San Francisco case in which a jury found a dog owner guilty of murder. In Canada, as the owner of a dog, you are responsible for its conduct. A dog may be considered a weapon. Simply put, if it kills someone, you are responsible and may be charged. There is also the issue of whether you have been cruel to the animal in training it to kill.

It's an offence under Section 443 to remove a boundary mark. In other words, it's against the law to tamper with or move those orange or red property markers that we have all seen. So, if you try to gain an extra inch of property, you could face five years in jail in a 12-foot by 12-foot cell.

As you'd expect, it's illegal to make or deal in counterfeit money. This is also covered in Part 12. Under Section 456, it's illegal to deface currency, so, when you place a penny on a railway track to produce a keepsake, you've committed a criminal offence.

A **weapon** is defined as:

any thing used, designed to be used or intended for use
(a) in causing death or injury to any person, or
(b) for the purposes of threatening or intimidating any person
and, without restricting the generality of the foregoing, includes a firearm.

As a result, a knife, gun, car or trained pet may be considered a weapon depending on its use.

Q: The police won't stop kids from cycling on sidewalks, and I've been hit getting off the bus. What can be done?

A: You may want to contact municipal enforcement officers. They may have taken over enforcement of this kind of activity (mischief, etc.), and that may be why the police won't get involved.

Q: My husband was charged along with a group of other motorcycle enthusiasts with not wearing a proper helmet. He is innocent and intends to fight the charge. Do you have any suggestions?

A: He or his lawyer should find out what evidence the Crown has against him. He may have been caught in a general crackdown on biker gangs and may well be innocent. Depending on the evidence gathered against him, he may want to hire a lawyer so that he isn't caught in this general crackdown. Any evidence in support of his case (i.e., his helmet) should also be preserved so that, if the case goes to trial, it is ready to be used.

Q: What happens if I buy a company that has committed a criminal offence, such as dumping toxic waste? Am I liable?

A: The company as the primary offender will be liable. Past directors and officers of the company can also be charged. As the current owner, you have a defence since you bought the company after the events occurred.

You may also have a civil recourse against the people who sold you the company since you didn't know about the criminal act.

Parts 12.1 and 12.2: Illicit Drug Use and the Proceeds of Crime

Part 12.1 of the Criminal Code works hand in hand with various other drug laws that regulate or outlaw certain drugs, such as heroin. Hence the focus in Section 462.2 that makes it illegal to import, export, manufacture, or promote instruments or literature for illicit drug use. Other aspects of drugs are covered in separate legislation.

Part 12.2 focuses on the proceeds of crime. While the drug itself is controlled by separate law, the code covers the proceeds from the drug trade. Part 12.2 also covers the proceeds from various criminal offences. For example, the proceeds from child pornography are covered in this section.

Detailed procedures are set out for search and seizure, court hearings, and forfeiture of property. These procedures ensure that a proper balance is struck between regulating criminal activities and protecting individual rights, including those guaranteed by the Charter of Rights and Freedoms.

PROCEEDS OF CRIME ACT, S.C. 2000 c. 17

In the summer of 2000, the government of Canada passed a separate Proceeds of Crime (Money Laundering) Act. It requires banks, accountants, and lawyers, among others, to report suspicious or large transactions to a new government agency called FINTRAC. Suspicious transactions are those in which a client seems to be unconcerned about the legal fees to be charged. Large transactions are those over $10,000.

Various groups have expressed concerns about the law, and some law societies have challenged it. They suggest that reporting every suspicious transaction to FINTRAC may breach solicitor-client confidentiality.

So, if a real estate client transfers $12,000 into a lawyer's account to cover real estate fees, this transaction should be reported to FINTRAC. Similarly, if you inherit $15,000 and deposit it into your bank account, your bank manager should report this transaction as well. The final regulations governing reporting have yet to be determined, and final challenges to the law have yet to be heard.

Q: My car was seized at the border. Can customs agents do that?

A: If your car was used in committing a crime, it's evidence that has to be kept until the end of the trial. It may also be forfeited if the police can connect its purchase to stolen money. This is called tracing the proceeds of crime from the cash to the purchase of some consumer item.

Part 13: Attempts and Conspiracies

This part of the Criminal Code deals with attempts and conspiracies. So, if you try to but don't kill someone, you won't be charged with murder; you'll be charged with attempted murder. If the offence that you tried to commit (the higher offence) carries a life sentence, then attempting to commit it carries a sentence of up to 14 years in jail. Similarly, if the higher offence carries a sentence of 14 years in jail, then attempting to commit it carries half that sentence, seven years. If you conspire with another person to commit murder, you will also be sent to jail for 14 years.

Historically, belonging to a union was illegal since unions were seen as restraining trade. Trade was essential to the British Empire, so if you conspired to restrict trade you'd be jailed. As workers gained more rights, unions were accepted, though initially in a very restricted capacity.

Hence, while Section 466 makes it illegal to restrain trade, a subsection allows unions to exist. The Supreme Court of Canada will soon consider when unions can sue or be sued, since once again their status in society is being debated.

"A conspiracy in **restraint of trade** is an agreement between two or more persons to do or to procure to be done any unlawful act in restraint of trade . . . (but a trade union is exempted)." As a result some employment agreements that prevent you from working in competition with your former employer, may be illegal as a restraint of trade.

Q: **Is a collection agency allowed to harass and threaten me about my student loan?**

A: Collection agencies are governed by provincial laws, which forbid them to threaten you, your boss, or your family. They can demand repayment and even sue you, but they can't threaten you. If they persist, they not only breach provincial law but also may commit a criminal offence since you can't threaten someone.

Q: **Our organization has an Internet mailing list. We've restricted access because we're worried that someone may misuse the list, say to stalk someone. Are we justified in doing this?**

A: Yes. The area of Internet law is expanding as the Internet itself expands. If the owner of a list acts imprudently and a person uses the list improperly, say by committing a criminal offence, both the owner of the list and the person abusing it can be held responsible both civilly and criminally. The key is whether the owner of the list acted reasonably and took the steps required to keep it secure.

Part 14: Jurisdiction

Once the Criminal Code has set out various offences, the next job of the law is to set out the jurisdictions of the courts. Hence, Section 468 states that every Superior Court in every province can hear most types of criminal trials. Certain offences, such as treason, must be dealt with in a higher court.

Since criminal activities can affect the life and liberty of a person, the law allows for jury trials. In this way, according to legal theory, you will be judged by your peers. You can opt out of a jury trial, but the attorney general (or his or her delegate) of your province must first agree.

What happens if you commit a criminal offence while on an aircraft anywhere in the world? Where will the trial take place — in which province or country? Section 476 tries to answer that question. The offence is deemed to have been committed either where the flight originated, over the territory where the aircraft flew, or at the flight's destination.

In other words, it's up to government lawyers to decide where the prosecution will occur, though if the accused is abroad he or she will have to be extradited to Canada.

Section 482 allows courts in each province to make procedural rules for trials, but the federal government retains the power to make rules that apply across the country.

Criminal Charges in the Court System

1. Charges are laid, and the trial takes place in the **Superior** or **Provincial Court**.
2. An appeal takes place in the **Court of Appeal**.
3. The final appeal takes place in the **Supreme Court of Canada**.

Q: Can I be charged in one province and have the trial in another?

A: Generally, the trial will occur in the province where the offence occurred. You can ask that the trial be moved to another province if you can show that you won't get a fair trial in the original jurisdiction. Otherwise, you can't change provinces. (If convicted, you can serve time in your own province on application to the court.)

In April 2002, the United Nations established the **International Criminal Court**, the ICC. This court is the first permanent tribunal mandated to deal with crimes committed during armed conflicts. The crimes include enslavement, torture, and rape. In the past, the UN has set up specific courts of law as in the Nuremburg trials, which dealt with crimes committed during the Second World War. Individuals who are now accused of these types of crimes will now be tried before the ICC.

Part 15: Special Powers

This part of the Criminal Code gives judges the power to dismiss cases because of various irregularities, and Section 486 gives them the power to exclude the public when it is in the interest of public morals to do so. It also provides for bans on publication. Bans, of course, are a constant source of legal challenge by media that want to publish information about a particular trial.

In determining whether to impose a publication ban, a judge must consider the following factors:
- the right to a fair hearing,
- the risk for the victim or a witness of intimidation or retaliation if his or her identity is disclosed,
- the interest of society in knowing about the offence,

- the alternatives that exist, and
- the impact of the ban on freedom of expression.

There are also special rules for child witnesses to ensure not only that they are protected but also that they understand the meaning of telling the truth.

Part 15 also deals with search warrants in Section 487 and the collection of forensic DNA. This section, like many others, works hand in hand with other laws, such as the DNA Identification Act. The section on DNA is detailed to ensure once again a balance between individual and societal rights.

Should execution of a search warrant lead to the seizure of information in the possession of a lawyer, and should that information be privileged or confidential, there are detailed rules in Section 488.1 to have the matter considered by a judge in a separate hearing. That judge, regardless of the outcome of the inquiry, will not preside over the subsequent trial since he or she has seen some of the evidence, privileged or not.

This part of the code then deals with the disposition of seized property, including in Section 491 the forfeiture of weapons and ammunition.

Q: Why are witnesses asked to leave the trial?

A: Witnesses are sent out of the courtroom to make sure that their testimonies don't influence those of other witnesses. This is distinct from a publication ban, which prevents the media from reporting on the trial until its conclusion.

FROM THE SUPREME COURT OF CANADA IN THE CASE OF DAGENAIS vs. CBC DECEMBER 8, 1994

The common law rule governing publication bans must thus be reformulated in a manner that reflects the principles of the Charter and, in particular, the equal status given by the Charter to ss. 2(b) and 11(d). Given that publication bans, by their definition, curtail the freedom of expression of third parties, the common law rule must be adapted so as to require a consideration of both the objectives of a publication ban, and the proportionality of the ban to its effects on the protected Charter rights. The modified rule may be stated as follows: a publication ban should only be ordered when (a) such a ban is necessary in order to prevent a real and substantial risk to the fairness of the trial, because reasonably available alternative measures will not prevent the risk; and (b) the salutary effects of the publication ban outweigh the deleterious effects to the free expression of those affected by the ban. . . .

Publication bans, however, should not always be seen as a clash between freedom of expression for the media and the right to a fair trial for the accused. The clash model is more suited to the American constitutional context and should be rejected in Canada. Other important concerns have a place at each stage of the analysis that is required when considering whether a particular publication ban can be justified under the common law rule. The efficacy of a publication ban is also a relevant factor on this analysis.

**FROM THE BC COURT OF APPEAL
IN THE CASE OF M.D. MINERALSEARCH INC.
vs. EAST KOOTENAY NEWSPAPERS LTD.
FEBRUARY 2002**

(Without a publication ban, issues can arise about reporting events that have occurred in court. For example, in December 1997, a local newspaper reported that the plaintiff M.D. Mineralsearch Inc. was found guilty of deceptive trade practices but omitted a statement by the presiding judge that the infraction was a minor clerical error. The plaintiff sued the newspaper for defamation and lost. The court found that the article was accurate but left a false impression. That in itself didn't warrant the awarding of damages.)

". . . [quoting the British Court of Sessions] where a newspaper merely purports to report the result of a case and does so with accuracy, it cannot be liable in damages if it fails to narrate the steps which led up to the judgement. . . . In my judgement there is no duty on a reporter in a report of a lawsuit to make his report exhaustive. It is, in my judgement, sufficient if the reporter gives the result of the litigation truly and correctly. . . ."

Parts 16 and 17: Appearance, Release, and Language

You can arrest anyone committing a criminal offence, anyone escaping custody, or anyone stealing your property. Take care, however, to ensure your own safety. Once you have arrested a person, you must take him or her to the police (Section 494). Once in the custody of the police, the person may be released with a written promise to appear in court (Section 496) or be kept in jail (Section 497) until the first appearance in court.

If arrested, you can be fingerprinted and photographed, though on being acquitted you can have these records destroyed. Also, once arrested and jailed, you'll generally appear before a judge within 24 hours. The judge will decide on the conditions, if any, of your release.

When someone is charged with a criminal offence, it's either because they have been caught in the act or because someone has complained about some activity and the police have investigated the matter. When the police find that an offence has been committed, they **lay an information** against the person, which can cause an arrest warrant to be issued. Anyone can lay an information. You don't have to be a police officer to do it. So, if you've complained to the police about some activity and they refuse to proceed, under Section 504 you can lay an information before a justice of the peace, who will hear the evidence. If the justice is convinced, charges will be laid, and the police will arrest the person.

After a person's arrest and first appearance in court, under Section 515 a judge can impose conditions on his or her release, which may include posting security or prohibiting the possession of firearms. Obviously, if he or she fails to appear at the next scheduled court date, an arrest warrant will be issued, and further release pending her subsequent trial will likely be refused.

A trial must take place within a reasonable time period. Depending on the offence, under Section 525, a trial must take place within 90 days of your first appearance in court. This is why you often hear of cases being dismissed without a trial: it's because a trial hasn't taken place within a reasonable time frame. Once the 90 days are up, though, you can't just walk out of jail. The matter must go before a judge, who may order your immediate release or, in certain cases, set a trial date outside the original 90-day period. It all depends on the charge and the circumstances of your case.

Part 17 guarantees your right to be tried in either French or English or, as the case may be, in any original Native language.

Q: As a Canadian, am I required to carry identification? Friends of mine were recently stopped for trespassing on private property. If they were arrested and failed to provide ID, would they be kept in jail until identified?

A: A series of laws need to be pieced together to answer this question. When driving a car, you have to carry ID in the form of a driver's licence and vehicle registration. When in a mall, you're on private property and must identify yourself to the mall owners or their security guards. A police officer has the right to ask you for ID if there are reasonable and probable grounds to stop you. While you don't need ID when walking down the street, if you walk your dog, he or she will have a dog tag that can be traced to you. It's therefore prudent to have some form of identification in case you're stopped. In some areas, there are also municipal loitering laws that require you to identify yourself. So, yes, if you are arrested, you can refuse to identify yourself until someone reports you missing or shows up with bail. If someone does so, you will be identified and may be charged with obstructing justice. Remember as well, if you make a phone call, with caller ID the police will be able to identify the person called and trace it back to you.

Parts 18, 19, and 19.1: Preliminary Inquiries, Trials without a Jury, and Nunavut

In some cases, a hearing is required to flesh out the charges and evidence for an upcoming trial. This is called a **preliminary inquiry**. In the United States, you often hear of a grand jury inquiring into some act. It's not quite the same since in the United States a panel hears evidence, while in Canada a judge does so.

But before you get to a preliminary inquiry, you'll be taken to court and asked under Section 536 whether you want to be tried by a judge alone or by a judge and jury, and whether you want a preliminary inquiry into your case. Lawyers often recommend these inquiries so that they can get a sense of the evidence against their clients.

The procedure to be followed at these inquiries is set out in the Criminal Code and is similar to a trial in which sworn evidence is obtained and assessed. At the end of the inquiry, the matter can be dismissed or proceed to a full-fledged trial.

In certain cases, lawmakers decide that a trial will take place without a jury. The matters are considered less serious, such as estate fraud under $5,000. However, if at any time during the proceedings it appears that a greater sum is at issue (Section 555), the matter can be bumped up to a trial with a jury.

Once the trial date has been set and you appear in court, you will be asked, as seen on TV, whether you plead guilty or not guilty. The answer is up to you.

Finally, since Nunavut is our newest territory created by law, Part 19.1 of the code defines the powers of the Nunavut Court of Justice and its judges. Otherwise, some lawyer might argue that the courts of that territory don't formally exist to try criminal matters and that all criminal charges should therefore be thrown out.

Q: Why should I agree to a preliminary inquiry?

A: You should agree to it to find out what evidence the police have gathered and what you'll need to prove in your defence.

Part 20: Jury Trials

With a jury, you are tried by your peers. But as we all know, when you receive a notice to serve on a jury, you think of every excuse to get out of becoming a juror. The most common excuse is that you have weak bowels and can't sit for more than an hour at a time. Since trials tend to last two days on average, you won't be able to serve as a juror. Being hard of hearing is also a good reason not to serve, though you should remember your civic duty.

This part of the Criminal Code deals with the rules and regulations governing jury trials. The government can request a jury trial and ask that some or all of the charges against you be tried at different times. It may want one charge dealt with and, depending on the outcome, drop other charges.

In selecting a jury, lawyers for the accused will try to pick jurors whom they think will be sympathetic to their case. The government lawyer, called the Crown prosecutor or **Crown**, will do the same thing. If you are charged with theft from your employer, your lawyer will try to find blue-collar workers who may have been mistreated by their bosses. The Crown will look for management people to serve on the jury since bosses will likely be hard on employees who steal. People who have been convicted of an offence will be disqualified; so will someone who, according to the wording of the code, "is an alien."

A jury is comprised of 12 people picked from voters' lists. Several hundred potential jurors are called to their local courthouse and convened in the largest room. Once the judge makes introductory remarks about the case to be tried, and potential jurors ask to be excused, the names of remaining potential jurors are placed in a drum and tumbled. From this drum, names are drawn and called out. A potential juror goes to the front of the court, and either the Crown lawyer or the defence lawyer can challenge that person's ability to serve. Depending on the charges laid, both lawyers can challenge up to 20 people. If you are challenged, you don't have to serve. If you aren't challenged, you are asked to sit in the jury box, and eventually you'll be sworn in to serve as a juror. If each lawyer uses up the number of challenges before 12 people are picked, then the next names called out automatically qualify.

Once the trial begins, the charge or charges will be read to you in open court. Under Section 581, the language used in the charge can be that of the section of the code or everyday language. Also, any missing detail in the charge is not a ground for its dismissal (Section 583). However, before a trial is set to begin, the Crown must disclose to your lawyer all the evidence it has against you. Under Section 587, if the Crown refuses or has given your lawyer only part of the information, the court can order that further details of the evidence be provided to ensure a fair trial.

The code deals with charges against several people who have committed the same offence and their right to have their trials joined together or separated. Under Section 599, you can ask that the location of the trial be changed if you think that media coverage or the potential pool of jurors will prevent a fair trial.

You will be asked how you wish to plead. You can plead guilty, not guilty, or say nothing, in which case the court will enter a not-guilty plea for you. You can also plead that you have already been tried for the offence. Using our historical roots, the code has a fancy term for that plea: **autrefois acquit** (already acquitted) or **autrefois convict** (already convicted). It's jargon for "been there, done that."

Section 620 deals with offences against companies. They can also be charged, and in a recent case a company was charged and brought into a battery (improper touching) case. Usually, only a living person can touch and hurt someone else. In this case, the company was charged since it had hired the person who'd allegedly assaulted an employee. The court found the company not guilty, but the case is significant in setting the precedent of charging a company as well with a criminal offence traditionally reserved for individuals.

In any trial, the Crown goes first, and the defence goes second. The jury will hear the evidence, and the judge will summarize the case before the jury withdraws from the courtroom to consider their verdict. While deliberating, the jury must be provided with food and accommodation (Section 647). Many a juror has held out on rendering a quick decision since a night in a hotel is a welcome break from the drudgery of home. The law also stipulates that the deliberation be confidential. Yet in a recent case, the Supreme Court of Canada opened the door to the possibility of a juror testifying in a rare and exceptional case.

Once the jury have reached a verdict, they will be brought back into the courtroom to render their decision. The judge will then thank them, and they will be discharged. If you are found not guilty, you too will be free to go. If you are found guilty, the judge will ask the lawyers for their arguments on sentencing. In some cases, the judge has no choice about the sentence; however, if there is a range of options, he or she will ask the lawyers for their views. The judge can order an assessment of you so that a proper sentence can be imposed. After the sentence, you will begin serving your time in jail, with credit given for the time already spent there.

Part 20.1, added to the code, deals with the power to order outside medical assessments. The often-heard phrase "not guilty on account of insanity" (the technical term is **"not criminally responsible on account of mental disorder"**) is set out by amendment as Section 672.34. If you are found not guilty because of your mental state, you will be sent to a specialized medical facility and released only on a thorough review by a special panel called a review board.

Q: If I'm found to be innocent, does the Crown have to pay for my legal fees?

A: Unlike in civil matters, where the winning side has its legal fees paid by the losing side, in criminal matters each side pays for its own legal fees. In rare cases, a judge, if convinced that the charge(s) should not have been brought, can order that part of the legal fees of the accused be paid.

FROM THE SUPREME COURT OF CANADA IN THE CASE OF R. vs. PAN JUNE 29, 2001

The proposition that the jury must deliberate in private, free from outside interference, is a principle that has deep roots in English common law. The common law rule of jury secrecy, which prohibits the court from receiving evidence of jury deliberations for the purpose of impeaching a verdict, similarly reflects a desire to preserve the secrecy of the jury deliberation process and to shield the jury from outside influences. Statements made, opinions expressed, arguments advanced, and votes cast by members of a jury in the course of their deliberations are inadmissible in many legal proceedings. In particular, jurors may not testify about the effect of anything on their or other jurors' minds, emotions, or ultimate decision. On the other hand, the common law rule does not render inadmissible evidence of facts, statements, or events extrinsic to the deliberation process, whether originating from a juror or from a third party, that may have tainted the verdict.

Evidence indicating that the jury has been exposed to some information or influence from outside the jury should be admissible for the purpose of considering whether there is a reasonable possibility that this information or influence had an effect upon the jury's verdict. Such evidence should be admissible regardless of whether it is a juror or someone outside the jury who offers the evidence. However, while jurors may testify as to whether they were exposed to extrinsic information in the course of their deliberations, the court should not admit evidence as to what effect such information had upon their deliberations. While jurors appropriately bring to their task their entire life's experiences, if a juror, or a third party, conveys to the jury information that bears directly on the case at hand that was not admitted at trial, by reason of an oversight or strategic decision by counsel or, worse yet, by operation of an exclusionary rule of admissibility, then it is truly a matter "extrinsic" to the deliberation process, and the fact that it was introduced into that process may be revealed.

Sample Notice to Serve on a Jury

Dear Prospective Juror:

Your name was selected at random from a municipal enumeration list to be considered for inclusion in a Jury Roll, which is a list of potential jurors. The Roll lists the names of citizens resident in a jurisdiction who, if summoned, would be eligible during the ensuing year to serve as jurors.

In order to prepare the Roll, your assistance and cooperation are required. You are required by law to fill out the enclosed questionnaire. Please read each question carefully to ensure that your answer is complete and accurate. Within five days, return the completed questionnaire using the enclosed, pre-addressed, postage-paid envelope.

Please note that receipt of this letter and completion of the questionnaire does not mean that you have actually been chosen to serve on a jury. Your eligibility to serve as a juror will be determined based on the answers you have provided to the questions in the questionnaire.

In conclusion, I want to stress that the jury system is one of the most important elements of our justice system. Jurors are responsible for determining, with the guidance of a judge, questions of fact in either civil or criminal court proceedings. Service as a juror is one of the most valuable contributions members of our society can make.

Thank you for contributing your time to this important endeavour.

Madame, Monsieur,

Nous avons extrait au hasard votre nom d'un recensement municipal en vue de le porter à la liste des jurés. Cette liste comporte les noms de personnes qui résident dans une localité donnée et qui, une fois convoquées, pourraient être admises à faire partie d'un jury au cours des douze prochains mois.

Nous vous saurions gré de bien vouloir nous aider à dresser la liste des jurés en répondant au questionnaire ci-joint, ainsi que la loi l'exige. Veuillez lire attentivement les questions afin d'y apporter des réponses exactes et complètes. Vous êtes prié(e) ensuite de retourner le questionnaire dûment rempli dans les cinq jours suivant sa réception en le glissant dans l'enveloppe pré-affranchie et pré-adressée ci-jointe.

Sachez par ailleurs que le fait de recevoir la présente lettre et de répondre au questionnaire ne veut pas dire que vous avez été effectivement choisi(e) comme juré. Votre admissibilité à faire partie d'un jury sera en effet détermine d'après vos réponses au questionnaire.

J'aimerais par la même occasion souligner que les proces devant jury constituent l'un des éléments les plus importants dans notre système judiciaire. C'est en effet au jury qu'il incombe, avec l'assistance du juge, de trancher les questions de fait en matière civile ou pénale. Les fonctions de juré comptent parmi les contri-butions les plus importantes que l'on puisse apporter à la société.

En vous remerciant d'avance du temps que vous consacrerez à cet aspect important de la vie en société, je vous prie de recevoir, Madame/Monsieur, l'expression de mes sentiments distingués.

FROM THE COURT OF APPEAL FOR ONTARIO IN THE CASE OF NELITZ vs. DYCK JANUARY 16, 2001

(The plaintiff sued her insurance company Gore and a treating physician. She alleged that she suffered battery at the hands of the doctor and that the company was also liable. Although she lost the lawsuit, the court discussed a company's potential liability for battery. Battery has traditionally been restricted to individuals.)

(3) Corporate liability for battery

In my view, the trial judge erred in finding that Gore could not be liable for battery because it was a corporation. While a corporation cannot itself commit battery, because it cannot physically touch an individual, in my view, it can be liable for battery directly by using an individual to commit the act, or vicariously for acts committed by an employee or agent within the scope of his or her authority. The trial judge considered only vicarious liability and dismissed the claim because Dr. Dyck was an independent contractor. However, if Mrs. Nelitz did not consent to the examination, Gore could be liable directly for battery because it expressly retained Dr. Dyck to commit the tort. There is no question that this form of liability was pleaded by the plaintiffs. In the statement of claim, the plaintiff alleged that Gore . . . "actively participated in the battery by encouraging or forcing Pauline Nelitz to undergo treatment by the Defendant, Dyck." Subject to the question of consent, there is also no doubt that Gore used Dr. Dyck to commit the alleged battery. Gore contacted Dr. Dyck, made an appointment and instructed Mrs. Nelitz to attend the examination.

Part 21: Appeals

If you are unhappy with the result of your trial, you can appeal it. This section of the Criminal Code sets out the rules for doing so. In some cases, a convicted person can be let out of jail pending the appeal. Appeals are often based on errors made by the presiding judge, and lawyers are adept at listing error after error, real or unreal. A lawyer sometimes keeps a separate scratch pad during a trial for this purpose. If the lawyer wins, he or she can throw out these notes. Judges are used to seeing long lists of errors in appeal documents. They have tough skins.

Under Section 686, the powers of the Court of Appeal are set out. A Court of Appeal can overturn the ruling of a lower court, confirm it as correct, or order a new trial. If you are still unhappy with the result, you can appeal to the Supreme Court of Canada. Section 691 allows for these appeals and has caused much debate in legal circles.

The reason for debate is that many more criminal matters get to that level of court than noncriminal matters since the test for the latter is more restrictive. Noncriminal matters must be of national importance to be heard. They are therefore less likely to reach the Supreme Court. Some argue that this is an unfair bias in favour of criminal matters. Others argue that they affect the liberty of a person, so all levels of our courts should consider them. Still others suggest that a separate final appeal court should be set up to resolve this issue. That concept was first proposed about 1984 but has yet to be accepted.

Section 690 gives the minister of justice power to order a new trial or to refer matters back to court. This section has recently gained prominence because it has been used for the wrongfully convicted.

Q: **After my appeal was heard, I uncovered some new evidence. Can my case be reopened?**

A: If the evidence was unavailable when the matter went to trial, and there was no way for you to know about it, then, yes, you can ask the courts to reopen the matter and consider the new evidence.

Q: **What does it mean when a court strikes out part of the Criminal Code?**

A: A court may find that a particular section of the code conflicts with existing law and is therefore illegal.

In that case, the section has no effect, and a charge brought under it must be dismissed. Often the section is declared unconstitutional, but the government is given, say, six months to fix it.

Parts 22, 23, and 24: Attendance, Sentencing, and Dangerous Offenders

Part 22 of the Criminal Code deals with subpoenas, which are a formal way of getting a witness into court. If a witness refuses to attend proceedings, a warrant for their arrest can be issued.

Part 23 deals with sentencing. When the government outlawed the death penalty, it decided to set out guidelines for and ranges of sentences for all criminal matters. Hence, Section 716 and following sections deal in great detail with sentences. Alternative measures are also allowed, and the most visible one involves the Native **sentencing circle**. In that case, the judge, the accused, the victim, and members of the community sit in a circle and discuss an appropriate sentence, which, if acceptable, forms part of the judge's ruling.

Section 718 states the purposes of sentencing as:

• denouncing the unlawful conduct,
• deterring the offender and others,

- separating where necessary the offender and society,
- rehabilitating the offender,
- providing reparation to the victim and society, and
- acknowledging the harm done.

In all cases, the sentence must fit the crime (Section 719).

The court has the power to hear impact statements from victims and to impose reasonable conditions, including fines (Section 734) or restitution orders under which the victim is compensated for the loss (Section 738).

If you are sentenced to two or more years in jail, you will serve your sentence in a federal prison (Section 743.1). If the sentence is less than two years, you'll end up in a provincial jail. The code then sets out when you can be released on what is called **parole**, subject to the original judge's sentence, which may have restricted your eligibility for parole.

Part 24 deals with dangerous offenders. Simply put, a dangerous offender is someone who has been found guilty of a serious crime, such as sexual assault, and remains a threat to the life, safety, or well-being of others — that is, he or she is likely to reoffend on release. A separate hearing is held to declare someone a dangerous offender, with the right to call evidence and the right to appeal any final ruling.

In Canada you can be **forced onto the witness stand** but some communications remain confidential. The law says:

> . . .the wife or husband, as the case may be, of the person so charged, is a competent witness for the defence . . .

But the law also says,

> No husband (or wife) is compellable to disclose any communication made to him (or her) by his wife (or husband) during their marriage . . .

Q: Can victims or community members give evidence not only of the impact of the crime but also when it comes to parole?

A: Yes, victims and community members have a role to play in both sentencing and parole. However, if prisoners have served their sentences, they are free to return to their home communities so that they can integrate back into society. Recent efforts by neighbours to block the return home of convicted individuals involve a fine balance (without an answer) between the rights of an individual and the community at large.

Victim Impact Statements

Statements from a victim are used by judges in imposing sentences. The information is also considered when the convicted person is being considered for parole.

According to a Correctional Services of Canada audit done in May 2001, only a third of these statements remain in a convict's file. Hence, parole officers are not always fully informed about an individual's criminal offence.

Experts

The other problem area is overuse of experts.

In some cases, the law becomes complex. Each side in a dispute may inevitably hire an expert to produce a report in favour of some argument to be advanced at the trial. The Crown may hire an expert to prove that fingerprints found at the scene of the crime could only have come from the accused. The defence may hire an expert to say that the accused has a rare skin condition that prevents his fingerprint from being unique. The judge may well get flustered.

The Supreme Court recently helped out beleaguered judges and brought experts down a notch or two. Judges now have a bit more leeway in discounting what experts have to say.

FROM THE SUPREME COURT OF CANADA IN THE CASE OF R. vs. J.-L.J. NOVEMBER 9, 2000

Expert witnesses have an essential role to play in the criminal courts. However, the dramatic growth in the frequency with which they have been called upon in recent years has led to ongoing debate about suitable controls on their participation, precautions to exclude "junk science," and the need to preserve and protect the role of the trier of fact — the judge or the jury. The law in this regard was significantly advanced by Mohan, supra, where Sopinka J. expressed such concern at p. 21:

> *Dressed up in scientific language which the jury does not easily understand and submitted through a witness of impressive antecedents, this evidence is apt to be accepted by the jury as being virtually infallible and as having more weight than it deserves.*

and at page 24:

> There is also a concern inherent in the appli-
> cation of this criterion that the experts not be
> permitted to usurp the functions of the trier of
> fact. Too liberal an approach could result in a
> trial's becoming nothing more than a contest of
> experts with the trier of fact acting as a referee
> in deciding which expert to accept.

. . . [T]he U.S. Supreme Court did list a number of
factors that could be helpful in evaluating the sound-
ness of novel science. . . .

> (1) whether the theory or technique can be and
>   has been tested:
>
> Scientific methodology today is based on
> generating hypotheses and testing them to
> see if they can be falsified; indeed, this
> methodology is what distinguishes science
> from other fields of human inquiry.
>
> (2) whether the theory or technique has been
>   subjected to peer review and publication:
>
> [S]ubmission to the scrutiny of the scientific
> community is a component of "good science,"

in part because it increases the likelihood that substantive flaws in methodology will be detected.

(3) the known or potential rate of error or the existence of standards; and,

(4) whether the theory or technique used has been generally accepted:

A "reliability assessment" does not require, although it does permit, explicit identification of a relevant scientific community and an express determination of a particular degree of acceptance within that community."

Parts 25, 26, 27, and 28: Recognizances, Extraordinary Remedies, Summary Convictions, and Forms

If you are charged and released, or if you are sentenced, you may have to promise to do certain things, such as returning to court on a given date or reporting to the police. When you promise to do so, it's called a **recognizance**. If someone posts money to guarantee your promise, he or she is called a **surety**. Part 25 defines these terms and allows for your arrest if you fail to fulfil your promise; it also allows for the forfeiture of the money posted by your surety.

In the olden days of kings, queens, and knights, you could be arrested and jailed unjustly without a trial. But as courts developed, procedures were put in place to have innocent people released from jail. Since Latin was frequently used in and around the royal court, it crept into the legal profession. Hence, we have the term **habeas corpus ad subjiciendum** or, in simple English, "deliver the person from illegal confinement." It actually became a separate law in England called the Habeas Corpus Act of 1862. Under that law, any judge of the realm could order the release of a person improperly detained anywhere in the realm, except if that person were on the Isle of Man. Habeas corpus is part of our law and is embodied in Part 26.

Part 27 deals with **summary convictions**, which by law are considered minor yet criminal offences. They are subject to fines of up to $2,000, to imprisonment for up to six months, or to both. The same safeguards for details of a charge, trials, sureties, releases, and appeals exist, but they are separated and dealt with in this part of the code.

Finally, the code sets out the forms required under criminal law. There are over 50 prescribed forms, which range from the form required when charges are laid to the form required when someone is detained in a health facility. If you are facing a criminal charge, these are the forms that you'll likely see.

- Form 6 — Summons
- Form 10 — Promise to Appear
- Form 16 — Subpoena

Form 6 — Summons

C A N A D A

Province of . . .

To A.B. of (place), (occupation):

Whereas you have this day been charged before me that (set out briefly the offence for which the accused is charged);

This is therefore to command you, in Her Majesty's name:

(a) to attend court on . . . , the . . . day of . . . A.D. . . . , at . . . o'clock in the . . . , at . . . or before any justice for the said (territorial division) who is there, and to attend thereafter as required by the court, in order to be dealt with according to law; and

(b) to appear on . . . , the . . . day of . . . A.D. . . . , at . . . o'clock in the . . . , at . . . , for the purpose of the Identification of Criminals Act. (Ignore if not filled in.)

You are warned that failure without lawful excuse to

attend court in accordance with this summons is an offence under subsection 145(4) of the Criminal Code.

Section 145(4) of the Criminal Code states as follows:

(4). Every one who is served with a summons and who fails, without lawful excuse, the proof of which lies with him, to appear at a time and place stated therein, if any, for the purpose of the Identification of Criminals Act or to attend court in accordance therewith, is guilty of

(a) an indictable offence and is liable to imprisonment for a term not exceeding two years; or
(b) an offence punishable on summary conviction.

Section 510 of the Criminal Code states as follows:

510. Where an accused who is required by summons to appear at a time and place stated therein for the purposes of the Identification of Criminals Act does not appear at that time and place, a justice may issue a warrant for the arrest of the accused for the offence with which he is charged.

Dated this . . . day of . . . A.D. . . . , at . . .

_____

A Justice of the Peace in and for . . . or Judge

Form 10 — Promise to Appear

C A N A D A
Province of . . .

I, A.B. of (place), (occupation), understand that it is alleged that I have committed (set out substance of offence).

In order that I may be released from custody,

1. I promise to attend court on . . . , the . . . day of . . . A.D. . . . , at . . . o'clock in the . . . , in courtroom No. . . . at court, in the municipality of . . . , and to attend thereafter as required by the court, in order to be dealt with according to law; and

2. I also promise to appear on . . . , the . . . day of . . . A.D. . . . , at . . . o'clock in the . . . , at (police station), (address), for the purpose of the Identification of Criminals Act. (Ignore if not filled in.)

I understand that failure without lawful excuse to attend court in accordance with this promise to appear is an offence under subsection 145(5) of the Criminal Code.

Section 145(5) and (6) of the Criminal Code state as follows:

(5). Every one who is named in an appearance notice or promise to appear, or in a recognizance entered into before an officer in charge, or another peace officer, that has been confirmed by a justice under section 508 and who fails, without lawful excuse, the proof of which lies with him, to appear at a time and place stated therein, if any, for the purpose of the Identification of Criminals Act or to attend court in accordance therewith, is guilty of

(a) an indictable offence and is liable to imprisonment for a term not exceeding two years; or

(b) an offence punishable on summary conviction.

(6). For the purposes of subsection (5), it is not a lawful excuse that an appearance notice, promise to appear or recognizance states defectively the substance of the alleged offence.

Section 502 of the Criminal Code states as follows:

502. Where an accused who is required by an appearance notice or promise to appear, or by a recognizance entered into before an officer in charge, or another peace officer to appear at a time and place stated therein for the purposes of the Identification of Criminals Act does not appear at that time and place, a justice may, where the

appearance notice or promise to appear, or recognizance has been confirmed by a justice under section 508, issue a warrant for the arrest of the accused for the offence with which he is charged.

Dated this . . . day of . . . A.D. . . . , at . . .

_____

(Signature of accused)

Form 16 — Subpoena

C A N A D A
Province of . . .

To C.D. of (place), (occupation):

Whereas A.B. has been charged that (state offence as in the information), and it has been made to appear that you are likely to give material evidence for (the prosecution or the defence);

This is therefore to command you to attend before (set out court or justice), on . . . , the . . . day of . . . A.D. . . . , at . . . o'clock in the . . . , at . . . to give evidence concerning the said charge and to bring with you anything in your possession or under your control that relates to the said charge, and more particularly the following: (specify any documents, objects or other things required).

Dated this . . . day of . . . A.D. . . . , at . . .

_____

A Judge, Justice or Clerk of the court

On April 17, 1982 Canada proclaimed a new Constitution that included a **Charter of Rights**. The Charter has had a profound effect on Canadians as it has caused, for example, individuals to be freed from jail and has caused laws to be struck down as unconstitutional. Here is a look at the news on April 17, 2002, the 20th anniversary of the Charter.

NEWS ITEM: U.S. set to unveil its plan to defend the continent . . . possible impact on Canada.
COMMENT: The U.S. plans a new defence strategy to replace NORAD. Canadians are concerned as it may erode their sovereignty by giving up their defence to the U.S. From a Charter perspective, some of these measures may well infringe on individual rights. The question is whether this restriction is for the benefit of society at large, in which case it would be ruled to be a reasonable restriction on individual rights.

NEWS ITEM: Man held 7 months, sent home with no ID.
COMMENT: A Canadian was held in a U.S. jail as a suspected terrorist. He was returned home without ID. In the post Charter era, he would be able to sue if there was no reasonable basis for his arrest.

NEWS ITEM: MPs have no say in how billions spent.
COMMENT: The Auditor General in her recent report criticized certain aspects of government spending. As a Canadian taxpayer, you have a right to have your money properly spent and accounted for. Your individual rights are therefore affected.

NEWS ITEM: Supreme Court in the spotlight in post Charter era.
COMMENT: On the anniversary of the Charter, the judges of the Supreme Court are under scrutiny. The debate is whether they have properly dealt with the Charter and whether they have gained too much power in using the Charter to strike down certain laws. Some argue that only elected officials can amend or repeal laws, and courts should not do so. Others argue that courts are there to provide a balance and check on our politicians.

NEWS ITEM: Ban on child porn struck down.
COMMENT: The U.S. Supreme Court struck down a child pornography law as unconstitutional. In Canada our Supreme Court upheld the Criminal Code provisions on child pornography yet allowed for an exception in the case of materials that have some artistic merit. Different countries have differing approaches.

Excerpts from the Charter of Rights:

Section 1: The Canadian Charter of Rights and Freedoms guarantees the rights and freedoms set out subject only to such reasonable limits prescribed by law as can be demonstrably justified in a free and democratic society.

Section 2: Everyone has the following fundamental freedoms: (a) freedom of conscience and religion; (b) freedom of thought, belief, opinion and expression, including freedom of the press and other media of communication; (c) freedom of peaceful assembly; and (d) freedom of association.

Section 7: Everyone has the right to life, liberty and security of the person and the right not to be deprived thereof except in accordance with the principles of fundamental justice.

Section 11: Any person charged with an offence has the right (a) to be informed without unreasonable delay of the specific offence; (b) to be tried within a reasonable time; . . . (d) to be presumed innocent until proven guilty according to law in a fair and public hearing by an independent and impartial tribunal . . .

COMMENT: These provisions establish the fundamentals of our democratic society. Many of these rights come from existing laws such as the 1960 Canadian Bill of Rights. These sections must as usual be read with other sections of the Charter and other laws. Our courts also add to this body of law. As an example, the right to a speedy trial is set out in the Charter and elaborated upon in the case known as Askov. Now when you're denied a speedy trial, your lawyer will raise the Askov defence. As a further example we have the principle of freedom of expression. While this is also a fundamental right, you can't libel or slander someone with your words or actions. These restrictions on your rights are justified by the last few words of Section 1.

There are many other rights set out in the Charter, such as mobility and equality rights. There are also rights set out in the Charter that give everyone basic legal protection in dealing with the justice system. They ensure fairness when criminal offences occur. For example you can't be forced to testify at your own trial, though you may wish to do so voluntarily to prove your innocence. The key is that the choice is yours and yours alone. The Charter guarantees that right. Also under Section 11 of the Charter, you are presumed innocent until proven guilty, a fundamental provision of our laws mirrored in Section 6 of the Criminal Code.

The Charter will remain an integral part of our law. Its role as a sword or shield in protecting rights may ebb and flow depending on the needs and rights of individuals as they come up against governments and organizations.

Conclusion

I hope that with this series of books, we have met the objective of providing basic information on questions that we all face when we come up against legal problems and issues. I hope that it will save you time and money when you need to consult a lawyer.

I also hope that you won't need to hire a lawyer, as it often means that you have a problem. Most matters can be resolved on your own by a letter or phone call. If not, then you *should* consult a lawyer, if only to clarify your rights. Then consider your options, as legal proceedings can be time consuming, emotionally draining, and costly.

For further information, your local courthouse will have pamphlets on basic rights, and the court staff is there to help you. Most government agencies are listed in the blue pages of your phone book. Courts and provincial law societies can be accessed on the World Wide Web. Use your favourite search engine and search for "court" or "law society" in your province. The Supreme Court of Canada has a web page located at www.scc-csc.gc.ca. Your local library will also have basic legal texts covering most areas of the law.

Thank you for using this book as a resource.

I hope that I have answered many of your legal questions. However, if your particular question needs to be answered or if there are follow-up issues that need to be addressed, you can write to me via the Internet by logging on to www.legalcounsel.ca.

Index

abortion, 30

abuse, 18, 33–35, 47

actus reus, 17

adult court, 5

Afghanistan, 7

age 12, 3, 5–6

age 14, 21–22

age 16, 23, 28, 33

aircraft, 3, 7, 47

anal intercourse, 21

appeals, 48, 66–67, 69, 75

assault, 29, 34

attempts, 45

autrefois acquit, convict, 59

balance of probabilities, 24

Bambi, 39

bars, 11

battery, 34, 59, 65–66

bawdy houses, 26

beachcomber, 35

bigamy, 30

boundary mark, 41

breaking and entering, 35

blood, testing, 29

breath, testing, 29

burden of proof, 23

Bush, President George W., 7

Charter of Rights and
    Freedoms, 15, 33, 43, 51,
    81–85

child witnesses, 50

church, 27

clergy, 21

collection agencies, 46

Constitution, 7, 31

conspiracies, 45

concurrent sentences, 13

counterfeit money, 41

criminal negligence, 28

criminal record, 8, 10, 27, 29

Crown, 5–6, 23, 27, 34–35,
    39, 42, 57–59, 61, 71

cruelty, animals, 40
customs, 45
cycling, 42

DNA, 1, 50
dangerous offender, 69
death penalty, 13, 19, 68
divorce, 33
drugs, 43
duelling, 7

England, 23, 75
Enron, 37
escaping custody, 17, 53
euthanasia, 4
experts, 39–40, 71–73
extradition, 18–19, 39

fingerprint, 10, 53, 71
firearms, 12–15, 54
first appearance, 54
forced witness, 70
forgery, 36
Forms 6, 10, 16, 76–81
fraud, 17, 37–38

gaming, 25, 27

Habeas Corpus, 75
hacking, 35
handgun, 15
helmet, 42

Heston, Charlton, 12
high treason, 6–8, 47
homicide, 28–29

identification, 54–55
ignorance, 3, 8, 17
indecent acts, 21
infanticide, 28–29
insanity, 60
interest rate, criminal, 35
International Criminal
    Court, 49
Internet, 46–47

John School, 27
jury trials, 40, 47, 56–63, 72

Kevorkian, Jack, 4
kidnapping, 29

lay an information, 53
Legal Aid, 12
legal fees, 61
libel and slander, 30, 33, 84
lie detector, 39
life sentence, 29–30, 45
lotteries, 25–26

mailing lists, 46–47
manslaughter, 28–29
mens rea, 17
motor vehicles, 29

murder, 2, 16, 24, 28–29, 40,
   45
mutiny, 7–8

new evidence, 67
NORAD, 81
Notice to Serve, 63–64

obstructing justice, 4
obscene materials, 21
oil rigs, 3
onus of proof, 14

parole, 30, 69–71
personate, 37
photograph, 24, 53
piracy, 7
plea bargaining, 34
polygamy, 30
Potter, Harry, 2, 36
preliminary inquiry, 55–57
presumption of innocence,
   14, 85
privacy, 23–24
prize fighting, 7–8
proceeds of crime, 43–45
property, 5, 14, 29, 35, 37, 43,
   50, 53, 55
prostitution, 26–27
publication bans, 49–52

rear-end collision, 9

reasonable doubt, 24
recognizance, 74
recording conversations,
   23–25
restraint of trade, 45–46
robbery, 3, 13, 35

sabotage, 7
search warrant, 14, 50
self-defence, 3
self-inflicted, 4
sentencing, 5, 30, 60, 68,
   70–71
sentencing circle, 68
sex and cars, 26
sexual assault, 29, 69
sexual intercourse, 4
sexual interference, 22
sexual offences, 21
shoplifting, 11
slot machines, 25–27
Smart, Maxwell, 19–20
space station, 3
spanking, 4
St. Laurent, Prime Minister,
   37
suicide, 3–5, 31–32
summary conviction, 75
surety, 75

tape, 23–25
theft, 35, 57

Three-Card Monte, 25
trial, 12, 16, 19, 34, 39, 42, 45,
    47–51, 54–56, 58–59, 65, 71,
    73, 75, 84–85

unions, 45–46
United Nations, 49

vacation clubs, 38–39
verdict, 59
victim impact statements, 69,
    71
videotape, 24

war, 38, 49

warnings, 9
weapons, 12–14, 40–41, 50
willfully intercepting, 24
wire, police, 25
wiretaps, 23
witchcraft, 35
World Trade Center, 7